Collection of Inter No-Bake & Flavored Cheesecakes!

Easy-to-Follow Collection of Mouth-Watering Cheesecake Recipes

BY: Nancy Silverman

COPYRIGHT NOTICES

© 2020 Nancy Silverman All Rights Reserved

Subject to the agreement and permission of the author, this Book, in part or in whole, may not be reproduced in any format. This includes but is not limited to electronically, in print, scanning or photocopying.

The opinions, guidelines and suggestions written here are solely those of the Author and are for information purposes only. Every possible measure has been taken by the Author to ensure accuracy but let the Reader be advised that they assume all risk when following information. The Author does not assume any risk in the case of damages, personally or commercially, in the case of misinterpretation or misunderstanding while following any part of the Book.

Table of Contents

Introduction 6

Chapter 1. Collection of International Cheesecake Recipes 8

    French Normandy Cheesecake 9

    South African Amarula Cheesecake 12

    Polish Sernik Cheesecake 14

    Swedish Cheesecake 17

    French Cheesecake 19

    Polish Krakow Cheesecake 22

    Lemon-Flavored German Cheesecake 25

    Japanese Cotton Soft Cheesecake 27

    Authentic German Cheesecake 30

    Greek, Yogurt Cheesecake 33

    English Passion Fruit & White Chocolate Cheesecake 36

    Italian Ricotta & Cream Cheese Cheesecake 39

    English, Lemon, Ginger & Lime Cheesecake 41

Korean Honey & Citron Tea Cheesecake 43

South African Buttermilk & Strawberry Cheesecake 46

New York Orange & Lemon Zest Classic Cheesecake 49

American Pumpkin Cheesecake 52

Swedish Almond Cheesecake with Strawberries & Mint 55

Strawberry Rhubarb Chicago Cheesecake 58

Chapter 2. Collection of No-Bake Cheesecake Recipes 62

Peanut Butter Cheesecake 63

Chocolate Cream Cheesecake & Amaretto 65

Apple Cheesecake 68

Peaches & Cream Cheesecake 70

Pistachio & Cherry Cheesecake 72

Chapter 3. Collection of Flavored Cheesecake Recipes 75

Pomegranate & Orange Cheesecake 76

Turtle Cheesecake with Brownie Base 78

Black Forest Cheesecake 81

Mixed Berry Cheesecake 83

Conclusion 86

About the Author 87

Author's Afterthoughts 88

Introduction

I am sure that you will delight in preparing this collection of both classic and rare of cheesecake recipes. Cheesecake is certainly on the top of my list of favorite sweet dish. Besides having so many different kinds of cheesecakes to try, it is really very simple and uncomplicated to prepare. Use my cheesecake recipes to help guide you into the world of preparing cheesecakes, then add your own special ingredients to them and explore and make them your own!

There is nothing better than being able to sit down with a friend or loved one and share a nice cup of tea or coffee served with a slice of your favorite cheesecake! You get to enjoy this special treat while exchanging stories and catching up with each other on your daily life experiences. Perhaps you can prepare your cheesecake with a friend or loved one or make a special cheesecake that you know they will love! You can surprise them by making a cheesecake to share with them. I am sure they will be delighted to no end getting to enjoy a yummy slice of cheesecake that was prepared especially for them!

In this collection of cheesecake recipes, I guarantee you that all of these cheesecakes will suit your personal tastes and those that are dining at your table. If you have dinner guests, you may want to prepare more than one selection of cheesecake for your guests—offering them an assortment of these easy-to-prepare dessert choices will leave them grinning with pleasure!

Chapter 1. Collection of International Cheesecake Recipes

French Normandy Cheesecake

A sweet treat that you are sure to savor every mouthful of!

Prep time: 20 minutes

Cook time: 40 minutes

Chill time: 2 hours

Servings: 12 persons

Ingredients:

For the crust:

- 1 teaspoon of vanilla extract
- 1/3 cup of sugar
- 1 cup of all-purpose flour
- 6 tablespoons of butter

For the filling:

- fresh raspberries for topping if desired
- 8 ounces brie cheese or Camembert, room temperature
- 2 eggs
- 2-8 ounces packs of light cream cheese, softened
- 1 teaspoon vanilla extract
- ½ cup sugar

Directions:

1. First, begin with heating your oven to 350° Fahrenheit.

2. For your crust, first, add the sugar and butter in a mixing bowl, then beat well, and add in vanilla.

3. Stir in your flour till it becomes crumbly.

4. Add your mix to a 9-inch spring-form pan and compress it down over the base and about an inch up the edges.

5. With a fork make holes over the base, then cook for about 15 minutes, or until it has set and is brown in color. Remove from oven and allow it to cool.

6. Prepare your filling, by adding the sugar with the butter in a bowl and beat together.

7. When the mix is smooth add the eggs, one at a time.

8. Remove any rind that might be on the cheese and cut into small pieces.

9. Place the rind into cheese mix and add the vanilla.

10. Pour mixture over the spring-form base.

11. Cook for 25 minutes.

12. Once it is set in the middle, take out of stove, and allow to cool.

13. Chill in the fridge for 2 hours.

14. Remove the spring-form and serve.

15. Top with fresh raspberries if you desire and enjoy!

South African Amarula Cheesecake

This cheesecake recipe is easy-to-prepare and is sure to delight your taste buds to no end!

Prep time: 30 minutes

Cook time: none

Chill time: 3 hours

Servings: 10-14 persons

Ingredients:

- 5 fluid ounces of amarula cream liqueur
- 5 ounces caster sugar
- 3 ½ ounces butter, melted
- 2 ¼ cups of soft cream cheese
- 7 fluid ounces whipping cream, extra cold
- 2 tablespoons dark chocolate, melted
- 7 ounces digestive biscuits
- 4 teaspoons gelatin powder

Directions:

1. Dissolve your butter and crush the biscuits and mix well in a mixing bowl.

2. Compress this mix into a 9-inch spring-form pan and place into freezer.

3. Beat your cream in another bowl until it begins to peak.

4. Add the gelatin and liqueur in another bowl and allow it to stand for 2-4 minutes.

5. Hold the bowl over boiling water until it has melted.

6. Beat the cheese with sugar in another bowl.

7. Add the gelatin to the mix, then add the cream gently.

8. Remove your spring-form pan from freezer and add the filling.

9. Dissolve your chocolate and drop small amounts of it on the top, take a cocktail stick and swirl it around.

10. Place it in the fridge for 5 hours, then remove when it is ready.

11. Slice cheesecake, serve and enjoy!

Polish Sernik Cheesecake

Enjoy this wonderful Polish Cheesecake. You can serve it with a cup of coffee!

Prep time: 45 minutes

Cook time: 1 hour

Servings: 12 persons

Ingredients:

For the crust:

- ¾ teaspoon of baking powder
- 2 large egg yolks
- ½ cup of sugar
- 3 tablespoons sour cream
- 2 cups all-purpose flour
- 5 ounces cold butter

For the filling:

- 2 pounds of dry curd cheese or quark cheese, sieved or put in a blender until smooth
- 2 cups of sugar
- 5 ounces butter, room temperature
- 1 teaspoon vanilla extract
- 4 large eggs, separated, at room temperature

Directions:

1. Heat your stove to 350° Fahrenheit.

2. Now for the pastry, add the sugar, butter, flour, and baking powder to your blender, then pulse mixture to form a dough.

3. In a bowl, blend the cream and egg yolks together.

4. Once cream mixture is done, add it to the flour mix, then pulse enough to combine well.

5. If the dough seems to be a bit on the dry side, then add another egg yolk to the mixture.

6. Spread butter around a 13 by 9-inch pan.

7. Roll your dough and place it in the pan including up the sides.

8. Make a pattern around the top edging of the pastry.

9. In a bowl, add your sugar and butter for the filling, and beat together so it becomes light and fluffy.

10. Now, beat in the vanilla, egg yolks, cheese, and combine well.

11. In another mixing bowl, whisk the whites of your eggs until stiff, then add to cheese mix.

12. Add the entire mix into your pastry base.

13. Place pan in the oven and cook for 1 hour.

14. Keep an eye on it as you do not want the top to brown.

15. Serve once the cheesecake is totally cool and enjoy!

Swedish Cheesecake

This is a cheesecake that will make for the perfect dessert at a family dinner!

Prep time: 10 minutes

Cook time: 1 hour

Servings: 6-8 persons

Ingredients:

- ¼ cup sugar
- 3-4 almonds, ground
- ¼ cup all-purpose flour
- 4 large eggs
- 1 tablespoon amaretto
- ½ cup oatmeal
- 24 ounces cottage cheese, drained

Directions:

1. Heat your stove to 425° Fahrenheit.
2. Beat your eggs in a mixing bowl, until they become light and fluffy.
3. Add the flour, cheese, and sugar, followed by the almonds and amaretto and mix well.
4. Grease a 9 by 13-inch casserole dish.
5. Add your cake mixture to pan and cook in your oven for 1 hour.
6. When cooking if top starts to color too fast, add a piece of tin foil to cover the top.
7. When done serve this cheesecake warm and enjoy!

French Cheesecake

This cheesecake recipe is perfect for serving with a light lunch!

Prep time: 20 minutes

Cook time: 45 minutes

Servings: 16 persons

Ingredients:

For the crust:

- ¼ cup granulated sugar
- ½ cup of flour
- ½ cup of unsalted butter
- ½ cup shortbread cookies, ground finely

For the filling:

- 1/3 cup granulated sugar
- 4 large eggs, separated
- ½ pound soft French cheese
- 1 tablespoon fine sugar
- ¼ cup heavy cream
- 1-pound cream cheese
- 1 teaspoon vanilla extract
- 1 tablespoon unbleached flour
- ¼ cup sour cream

Directions:

1. Heat your stove to 350° Fahrenheit.

2. Place your crust ingredients into your blender and pulse until they are well combined and fine.

3. Compress this mix into a 9-inch greased spring-form pan.

4. Next, cream your heavy cream and cream cheese, then beat in the flour with the sugar.

5. Once mixed, add your two creams, egg yolks, and vanilla.

6. Whisk your egg whites with the fine sugar until it begins to peak, then carefully add it to the cheese mix.

7. Add the mixture to your spring-form pan and cook for 45 minutes.

8. Once the center of your cheesecake is solid, remove it from the oven and allow it to cool. Serve and enjoy!

Polish Krakow Cheesecake

This tasty cheesecake will have you coming back for more!

Prep time: 10 minutes

Cook time: 45 minutes

Chill time: 1 hour

Servings: 10 persons

Ingredients:

For the crust:

- 2 ¾ cups plain flour
- 1 cup castor sugar
- 1 ¾ cups unsalted butter, softened
- 1 egg, plus 1 extra, beaten egg for brushing

For the filling:

- 1 orange, zested fine
- ¾ cup sour cream
- 5 eggs, plus 5 extra yolks
- ½ cup plain flour
- 3.3 pounds polish cottage cheese
- ¾ cup sultanas
- 1 cup castor sugar

Directions:

1. Beat your butter and sugar in a bowl for the pastry.

2. Sift your flour into the butter mix, and form a dough, then divide it into one third and two thirds.

3. Roll out the two thirds on a worktop with flour until it is ½ inch thick and lay it into a 9-inch spring-form pan.

4. Place in the fridge for an hour.

5. Now take the one-third piece of dough and mix in the egg, and flatten out into a disk shape, wrap some cling film around it and store it in the fridge.

6. Heat your oven to 350° Fahrenheit, then remove the spring-form pan from the fridge and use a fork to make holes in the base of the pastry.

7. Place into the oven and cook for 12-15 minutes, or until golden, then remove and allow it to cool.

8. Flour the work top again and roll the one third pastry out until it is ¼ inch thick.

9. Cut into long strips and place back into the fridge.

10. Blend the filling ingredients with the cheese and half of the sugar in a mixing bowl.

11. Add the cream, orange zest, and sultanas and mix well to combine.

12. Use another bowl to beat the rest of the sugar with the egg yolks and eggs. Gently mix into the cream mix.

13. Add the flour and mix well, then ladle into the base of the spring-form pan.

14. Crisscross the pastry strips over the top and egg wash the top.

15. Set in your oven and bake for 35-40 minutes.

16. Once the cake has set, remove it from the oven and allow it to cool. Serve and enjoy!

Lemon-Flavored German Cheesecake

This is a German cheesecake that you are sure to enjoy!

Prep time: 10 minutes

Cook time: 3 hours

Servings: 8-10 persons

Ingredients:

- ½ teaspoon vanilla extract
- 3 tablespoons cornstarch
- 4 eggs
- 2-8 ounces cream cheese packs
- 2 tablespoons fresh lemon juice
- 1 ½ cups sugar
- 1-pint sour cream
- 1-pound ricotta cheese
- ¼ cup melted butter
- 3 tablespoons flour

Directions:

1. Beat your two kinds of cheeses, then add the eggs and sugar to mix and beat again.
2. Add the cornstarch, vanilla, lemon juice, and flour and then beat until smooth.
3. Blend in your cream and butter until well combined.
4. Grease a 9-inch spring-form pan with butter.
5. Pour mixture into pan and place into the oven.
6. Turn on the heat to 325° Fahrenheit and cook for 70 minutes.
7. When the cake is done, turn off the heat and leave in the oven for 2 hours.
8. Use a topping of your choice for your cheesecake, then serve and enjoy!

Japanese Cotton Soft Cheesecake

You are sure to enjoy this delightful tasting Japanese cheesecake!

Prep time: 30 minutes

Cook time: 70 minutes

Servings: 10 persons

Ingredients:

- 9 ounces cream cheese
- 6 egg yolks
- ¼ teaspoon cream of tartar
- ¼ teaspoon salt
- 2 ounces unsalted butter
- 2 ounces cake or superfine flour
- 1-ounce cornflour
- 6 egg whites
- 1 tablespoon lemon juice
- 3 fluid ounces fresh milk
- 5 ounces fine granulated sugar

Directions:

1. Preheat the stove to 325° Fahrenheit, grease an 8-inch cake tin, then add greased parchment paper.

2. Using a bowl over hot water, dissolve your butter, cheese, and milk together, then cool slightly.

3. Mix in the salt, flour, lemon juice, egg yolks, and corn flour.

4. In another bowl, beat your egg white and tartar together when it becomes slightly stiff add in the sugar.

5. When it forms peaks, it is ready.

6. Gently mix ¼ of the egg white into your cheese mix, then mix in another ¼ of the egg white.

7. Add the cheese mix to the rest of the whites.

8. Place the mix into your prepared cake pan, then set the pan into a baking dish with some water in the bottom.

9. Cook for 70 minutes, remove from oven when done, or it is golden brown all over and is set in the middle.

10. Allow to cool, then serve and enjoy!

Authentic German Cheesecake

Treat yourself to this flavorful German cheesecake!

Prep time: 25 minutes

Cook time: 70 minutes

Servings: 8 persons

Ingredients:

For the base:

- 6 ounces of butter
- 2 medium eggs
- ½ ounce vanilla sugar
- 6 ounces sugar
- ½ ounce baking powder
- ¾ lb. Flour

For the filling:

- ½ ounce vanilla sugar
- 2 tablespoons sugar
- lemon zest
- 1 cup heavy cream
- 3 egg yolks, separated, the whites beaten to peak
- ½ cup sugar
- 1 cup light sour cream
- ½ ounce vanilla pudding
- 1-pound low-fat quark or 2-8-ounce packs cream cheese

Directions:

1. Heat your stove to 375° Fahrenheit.

2. To prepare the base, blend the ingredients together.

3. When you have prepared the dough, lay in the spring-form pan, including the sides.

4. Cook in the oven for 10 minutes at 375° Fahrenheit, then allow to rest and cool.

5. Blend your sugar and cream, along with sugar vanilla sugar, and cheese, when it becomes creamy beat in the egg yolks.

6. In a different bowl, stir the pudding powder, sugar, and a little cream, once mixed add the rest of the cream.

7. Add the pudding mix to your cheese mix and blend to combine well.

8. Mix in the peaked egg white.

9. Add the whole mixture into the spring-form pan and cook for an hour in your oven.

10. For the remaining 10 minutes of cook time, place a piece of parchment paper over the top.

11. When finished, it should be a light brown or golden color.

12. Remove from the oven and allow the cake to cool in pan.

13. Slice, serve and enjoy!

Greek, Yogurt Cheesecake

Your loved ones will be sure to enjoy this yummy Greek treat!

Prep time: 20 minutes

Cook time: 1 hour

Chill time: 2 hours

Servings: 10 persons

Ingredients:

- Kosher salt to taste
- 8-ounces reduced-fat cream cheese
- 2 tablespoons unsalted butter, melted
- ¼ cup all-purpose flour
- 1-17 ounce plain Greek yogurt
- 1 teaspoon lemon zest, finely grated
- 2 cups wild frozen blueberries
- 2 cups cinnamon sugar pita chips, crushed
- 3 large eggs
- 1 teaspoon unflavored gelatin
- ¾ cup sugar
- ¾ cup of unsweetened pineapple juice
- cooking spray
- 1 teaspoon vanilla

Directions:

1. Heat your stove to 325° Fahrenheit and place the rack in the middle of the stove.

2. Grease a 9-inch spring-form pan, using cooking spray, place tin foil around the base and edges, now sit it onto a baking tray.

3. Use a blender to pulse the chips into crumbs, then mix in the butter.

4. Compress the mix into the spring-form pan, over the base, and up the sides, halfway.

5. Cook in your stove for 4-5 minutes or just to dry them out a little.

6. Mix the eggs, vanilla, yogurt, ½ teaspoon salt, zest, sugar, and flour, then place into a blender and combine until smooth.

7. Once it is smooth, add to the spring-form pan and cook for 50 minutes in a stove.

8. When ready, place cake onto a cooling rack, once cool, place it in the fridge for 3 hours.

9. Add the pineapple and berries to the pan, heat until it begins to boil, then give it 5 minutes to cook before turning off the heat.

10. Blend the gelatin with 1 tablespoon of water and leave to the side.

11. After about 4-6 minutes, add it to the fruit mix.

12. Place into bowl and allow it to chill for 3 hours.

13. When the cake is done, take it from the spring-form pan and spread the topping over it.

14. Slice, serve and enjoy!

English Passion Fruit & White Chocolate Cheesecake

This is an English cheesecake recipe that will leave you feeling very satisfied!

Prep time: 30 minutes

Cook time: 75 minutes

Chill time: 5 hours and 15 minutes

Servings: 9 persons

Ingredients:

- ½ cup passion fruit pulp
- ½ cup single cream
- 4 tablespoons butter, melted
- 6 passion fruit, pulp removed
- 3 egg whites
- 1 cup Mascarpone cheese
- 3 egg yolks
- 4 tablespoons icing sugar, for dusting
- 4 tablespoons caster sugar
- 4 ounces white chopped chocolate
- 1 cup soft cream cheese
- 3 ½ ounces of crushed digestive biscuits
- 1 tablespoon butter, melted

Directions:

1. Heat your oven to 300° Fahrenheit and rub 1 tablespoon of dissolved butter around a 9-inch spring-form pan.

2. Blend 4 tablespoons of butter with cookie crumbs.

3. Once crumbs are smooth, compress into the spring-form pan, and place in the fridge to set.

4. Dissolve the chocolate in a mixing bowl that is placed over a pan of hot water, stir until smooth then set aside.

5. In a large bowl, beat the cheeses until they are smooth, then add in your egg yolks and sugar.

6. Mix in the passion fruit pulp with the chocolate.

7. Use another bowl, whisk the egg whites until it forms peaks.

8. Mix in the one-third of the white mix to the chocolate mix, mix well.

9. Mix in the remaining whites until there are no streaks in your mix.

10. Add the mix to your spring-form pan and sit on a baking tray.

11. Cook for 75 minutes, or until the cake becomes solid in the middle.

12. Turn off your oven and open the door, leave the cake in the oven for 3 hours.

13. Once the cake is cooled, place in the fridge, and allow it to chill for 2 hours.

14. When you are ready to serve your cheesecake, remove it from the pan onto a serving platter, leaving it at room temperature for 30 minutes.

15. Dust with sugar and serve it with the pulp of the 6 passion fruits and enjoy!

Italian Ricotta & Cream Cheese Cheesecake

If you are in the mood for a sweet Italian dish, then I would suggest you try this recipe!

Prep time: 15 minutes

Cook time: 2 hours

Chill time: 4 hours

Servings: 8 persons

Ingredients:

- 3 tablespoons cornstarch
- 1 ½ cups white sugar
- 1 teaspoon lemon juice
- 1-16 ounce container ricotta cheese
- 1-pint sour cream
- 2-8 ounces packs cream cheese, softened
- ½ cup melted butter, cooled
- 1 teaspoon vanilla extract
- 4 eggs

Directions:

1. Heat your stove to 350° Fahrenheit and rub the butter around in a 9-inch spring-form pan.

2. Blend your cheeses together, using a bowl.

3. Mix in your lemon juice, sugar, flour, eggs, butter, cornstarch, and vanilla.

4. Combine well, then add the cream last, place into your spring-form pan.

5. Cook for 1 hour in your oven, once cake is done, turn off your oven, and leave the cake in the oven for 1 hour with the door open.

6. Transfer the cake to your fridge and allow it to cool completely.

7. Serve and enjoy this tasty Italian cheesecake!

English, Lemon, Ginger & Lime Cheesecake

Enjoy this mouth-watering tasty English cheesecake. You can eat it with a nice cup of tea!

Prep time: 30 minutes

Cook time: 20 minutes

Servings: 4 persons

Ingredients:

- 2 lemons, juiced
- sliced kiwi, passion fruit, and mango
- 3/8 cup of hot water
- 6 tablespoons sugar
- 1 sachet of gelatin
- ¾ cup crumbled ginger biscuits
- 1 cup extra light cream cheese
- 1 teaspoon lemon extract
- 1 fresh lime, juiced
- ¼ cup butter, melted
- ¾ cup evaporated milk, chilled

Directions:

1. Blend the crushed biscuits with the melted butter, then compress into an 8-inch spring-form a pan.

2. Place in your fridge to chill.

3. Melt the gelatin by using the hot water, add to a bowl with the lime and lemon juice, set aside to rest.

4. Whisk the evaporated milk until it becomes thick.

5. Next, beat the vanilla, lemon extract, cheese in a different bowl.

6. Add your sugar into the lemon mix, then stir into the cheese mix.

7. Gently add your mix into the spring-form pan and set in your fridge overnight to set.

8. Top with sliced fruit before serving and enjoy!

Korean Honey & Citron Tea Cheesecake

This Korean cheesecake recipe is sure to delight your dinner guests to no end!

Prep time: 35 minutes

Cook time: none

Chill time: 3 hours

Servings: 6-8 persons

Ingredients:

For the filling:

- 1 tablespoon lemon juice
- 1 tablespoon gelatin
- ¼ cup fresh milk
- 3 tablespoons sugar
- 3 tablespoons water
- 2 ¼ cups cream cheese
- 3-4 tablespoons of Korean honey citron tea paste
- 1 cup non-dairy topping cream

For the crust:

- 6 ounces Marie biscuits, crushed
- 3 ½ ounces butter, melted

For the topping:

- 5 ½ tablespoons of Korean honey citron tea paste
- 1 ½ teaspoons gelatin, mixed with 2 tablespoons of water

Directions:

1. First, line a 9-inch spring-form pan, then set aside.
2. Blend the crumbs and butter in a bowl and mix well.
3. Compress the biscuit mix around your pan bottom and place in your fridge.
4. Next, prepare your filling by dissolving the gelatin in water in a bowl.
5. As it begins to swell, place over boiling water, and stir once then allow to cool.
6. Now, beat your cream for the topping and place it to the side.
7. Using another bowl, cream the cheese and sugar together, so it becomes light and fluffy.
8. Slowly add your milk to the mix and blend well.
9. Add the tea paste, gelatin, and lemon juice, then stir well.
10. Blend in the whipped cream and mix.
11. Add the mix to the spring-form pan, level it out and place in your fridge for 4 hours.
12. When making your topping dissolve your gelatin as the same method above.
13. Blend in the tea paste and allow it to cool down.
14. Smear mix over your cheesecake.
15. Keep your cheesecake in your fridge until you are ready to serve and enjoy it!

South African Buttermilk & Strawberry Cheesecake

Give yourself and your loved ones a special tasty treat and prepare this South African cheesecake recipe!

Prep time: 30 minutes

Cook time: none

Chill time: 2 hours

Servings: 8-10 persons

Ingredients:

For the crust:

- 1-7 ounce pack of shortbread biscuits
- 3 ½ ounces unsalted butter, melted

For the filling:

- 1 cup cultured buttermilk
- 1 small lemon, zested
- 1/3 cup water
- 1 teaspoon pure vanilla extract
- 1 cup cream
- 4 teaspoons powdered gelatin
- 1 cup caster sugar
- 1-9 ounce tub cream cheese

For the topping:

- 2 tablespoons water
- 1 teaspoon powdered gelatin
- 1 quart of fresh strawberries
- lemon juice and caster sugar to taste

Directions:

1. Place your biscuits in your blender, and pulse until they become crumbs.

2. Add biscuit crumbs to a bowl, then blend with melted butter and mix well.

3. Spread some more butter over a 9-inch spring-form pan, place inside cling wrap, and spread butter again.

4. Place the edges of your cling wrap under the pan.

5. Compress the biscuit mixture on the bottom of the pan and around the sides, then place in your fridge to chill.

6. Make your filling by melting the gelatin in water over hot water in a bowl once it becomes clear to remove and allow it to cool.

7. Beat your cheese and ½ of the buttermilk in a bowl, then once it is smooth, add the remaining buttermilk, vanilla sugar, and zest.

8. When the mixture is smooth, add in the gelatin.

9. In a different bowl, beat the cream, so it forms peaks, then add the cheese to this mix.

10. Place mixture on top of your crust base and place in the fridge for 3 hours.

11. Meanwhile, dissolve gelatin the same way as mentioned above.

12. Place your strawberries into a blender, add sugar to your taste and pulse into a puree.

13. Take 1 cup of your strawberry mix and add in 2-3 drops of lemon juice and mix in the gelatin well. Spread mixture over the top of your cheesecake and place it back in the fridge to chill.

14. To remove your cake from the pan, heat the sides and remove using a pallet knife.

15. Place the cheesecake on a platter, then slice, serve and enjoy!

New York Orange & Lemon Zest Classic Cheesecake

This New York-style cheesecake is sure to have you coming back for a second slice!

Prep time: 30 minutes

Cook time: 75 minutes

Chill time: 8 hours

Servings: 8-12 persons

Ingredients:

For the crust:

- ¼ teaspoon salt
- ½ vanilla bean, cut deseeded and kept
- 8 tablespoons unsalted butter, diced
- 1 egg yolk
- 1 cup flour
- 1 teaspoon lemon zest

For the filling:

- 1 ¼ cups sugar
- ½ teaspoon vanilla extract
- 3 tablespoons flour
- 1 ½ teaspoon orange zest
- 5 eggs, plus 2 extra yolks
- 2 ½ pounds cream cheese, softened
- 1 ½ teaspoons lemon zest
- ¼ cup heavy cream

Directions:

1. To prepare your crust, blend all of your crust ingredients in a bowl together.

2. Rub the mixture together with your hands to form a dough.

3. Divide your dough into two and chill for 1 hour, with each piece wrapped in cling film.

4. Place one piece of your dough into the base of a 9-inch spring-form pan and compress it down, use the other piece for the sides, pressing it down to secure.

5. Heat your stove to 500° Fahrenheit.

6. Now, using the mixer or hand blender, beat your cream cheese, flour, vanilla, zest, and sugar until it becomes smooth.

7. Add your eggs one at a time, and the yolks until smooth and creamy.

8. Blend in your cream and then add to your spring-form pan.

9. Place the pan into your oven, cook for about 15 minutes, or until it starts to color, then turn down the heat.

10. Cook for an additional hour with the heat set at 200° Fahrenheit.

11. Once the cake is done, remove it from the oven and place it on a cooling rack for 30 minutes.

12. Place a cover over the cake and put it in the fridge to chill for 8 hours.

13. Remove cake from spring-form pan, then slice, serve and enjoy!

American Pumpkin Cheesecake

For all of the pumpkin lovers out there, you will certainly enjoy this American pumpkin cheesecake!

Prep time: 20 minutes

Cook time: 45 minutes

Servings: 10-12 persons

Ingredients:

- ½ cup heavy cream
- 1-pound pumpkin puree
- 1 cup brown sugar
- 4 eggs
- ½ teaspoon nutmeg
- 1-pound cream cheese
- 1 cup bread crumbs
- 1 teaspoon cinnamon
- vanilla ice cream for serving if desired
- 1 teaspoon vanilla
- 1 pound of ricotta cheese

Directions:

1. Heat your stove to 325° Fahrenheit.

2. Spread the butter around the inside of a 9-inch spring-form pan and place parchment paper inside the pan.

3. Blend the sugar and cream cheese in a bowl together.

4. Once the cream cheese mixture is smooth, add the spices, along with the cream, then puree to it is combined well.

5. Once the mixture is creamy, stir in your crumbs with the eggs, one at a time.

6. Blend in the ricotta cheese.

7. Add the cake mix to your prepared cake pan.

8. Cook cake in your oven for 45 minutes.

9. When it is ready to take out of the oven, cool and then serve with vanilla ice cream and enjoy!

Swedish Almond Cheesecake with Strawberries & Mint

Serve this tasty Swedish cheesecake recipes to your loved ones for a special treat!

Prep time: 30 minutes

Cook time: 1 hour

Servings: 8 persons

Ingredients:

- ¾ cup milk
- ¾ cup heavy cream
- 2 ¼ cups cottage cheese, drained overnight
- ½ cup mint, minced
- ¾ cup sugar
- whipped cream for finishing
- 6 cups strawberries, quartered
- 3 eggs
- ¾ cup blanched almonds
- unsalted butter, for greasing
- ¼ cup flour
- confectioner sugar for garnish

Directions:

1. Mix the strawberries, mint, 1/3 cup sugar in a bowl, then allow to rest for an hour.

2. Next, heat your oven to 350° Fahrenheit and spread the butter over an oval 3-quart baking tray, then set to one side.

3. Add the almonds and remaining sugar into your blender and pulse until ground finely.

4. Mix in the milk, cottage cheese, eggs, cream, and flour, then pulse again until smooth.

5. Add your mixture to the baking tray, then cook until it becomes puffed up and golden, after about 45 minutes to 1 hour in the oven.

6. Remove the cake from the oven, and allow it to cool, then sprinkle confection sugar on top.

7. Serve along with strawberries and cream, then enjoy!

Strawberry Rhubarb Chicago Cheesecake

Treat yourself a nice slice of this Chicago style cheesecake!

Prep time: 25 minutes

Cook time: 70 minutes

Chill time: 3 hours

Servings: 10-12 persons

Ingredients:

For the crust:

- 6 ounces of graham crackers
- ¼ teaspoon nutmeg, fresh, grated
- 5 tablespoons unsalted butter, melted, plus a bit for greasing
- ¼ teaspoon kosher salt
- 1 teaspoon sugar

For the filling:

- ½ cup sour cream
- 1 vanilla bean, cut in two and deseeded, keep the seeds
- 2 tablespoons dark rum
- 1 ½ pounds of rhubarb, trimmed and sliced into ¼-inch thick pieces
- 2 tablespoons fresh lemon juice
- 1 ½ cups sugar
- charred rhubarb compote
- 2 tablespoons unsalted butter, softened
- 4 eggs, room temperature
- 3-8-ounce packs of softened cream cheese
- ½ teaspoon kosher salt
- sliced strawberries for garnish

Directions:

1. Heat your oven to 375° Fahrenheit. Spread butter into a 9-inch spring-form pan.

2. Add your crackers to your blender and pulse until they are crumbs.

3. Mix with the nutmeg, melted butter, sugar, salt and combine well.

4. Compress the mix into your spring-form pan and up the sides.

5. Cook in the oven for about 9-minutes to set, then remove from oven and cool. Place some foil around the spring-form pan and set it on a baking dish.

6. Turn down the stove to 325° Fahrenheit.

7. Add your cream cheese and cream together in a bowl, then beat until smooth.

8. Add the butter and sugar and mix again.

9. Add in your eggs one by one and blend well.

10. Add the vanilla, rum, salt, and vanilla seeds, and mix then add to the spring-form pan.

11. In your roasting tray, add some boiling water, enough to reach halfway up spring-form pan and place in oven for 55 minutes.

12. Remove cake from spring-form pan and allow it to cool down, then place it in the fridge for 4 hours.

13. Spread the rhubarb compote, over the cake and finish with strawberries.

14. For your compote you will need to heat your broiler.

15. Layout your rhubarb onto a baking tray, which has been greased.

16. Cook for 8 minutes to char rhubarb, then add to the pan.

17. Add the rest of the ingredients apart from the lemon juice, and cook until it becomes jam-like, around 25 minutes.

18. Now remove from heat and add the juice and cool, remove the vanilla pod, and you are ready to spread over top of cheesecake.

19. Slice, serve and enjoy!

Chapter 2. Collection of No-Bake Cheesecake Recipes

Peanut Butter Cheesecake

Satisfy your peanut butter craving with this yummy no-bake peanut butter cheesecake recipe!

Prep time: 20 minutes

Cook time: none

Chill time: 2 hours

Servings: 12 persons

Ingredients:

- ¼ cup butter, melted
- 2-8 ounces packs of cream cheese, softened
- 2 bars Swiss milk chocolate, chopped fine and divided
- 1 cup smooth peanut butter
- 1 ¼ cups Oreo baking crumbs
- 1 ¼ cups thawed cool whip, divided
- 1 cup sugar

Directions:

1. Blend the butter with the crumbs and compress into a 9-inch spring-form pan.

2. Place in your fridge for 10 minutes to chill.

3. Cream the peanut butter, cheese, and sugar.

4. Stir in ½ of the chocolate and blend together.

5. Beat 1 cup of cool whip and mix in gently.

6. Place in your fridge for 2 hours.

7. Place the rest of the chocolate with the cool whip and microwave for 60 seconds on high.

8. Spoon the hot mixture over the top of your cheesecake and keep in the fridge to allow it to set.

9. Remove from spring-form pan and place on a serving platter, slice, serve and enjoy!

Chocolate Cream Cheesecake & Amaretto

Whip up this delightful Chocolate cream cheesecake for a yummy sweet treat!

Prep time: 40 minutes

Cook time: none

Chill time: 2 hours

Servings: 8-10 persons

Ingredients:

- 2 cups heavy cream
- 6 tablespoons unsalted butter, melted
- 12 fresh large ripe strawberries
- 12 ounces milk chocolate morsels
- 6 tablespoons amaretto liqueur
- 16 ounces chocolate chip cookies, ready to eat
- 2 cups cream cheese, room temperature
- 12 ounces semi-sweet chocolate morsels
- 1 ½ sour cream
- 1/3 cup granulated sugar
- 1 teaspoon vegetable oil
- 12 strawberries, fresh and ripe

Directions:

1. Cut out a round piece of parchment paper to fit the base of a 9-inch spring-form pan, then rub grease round the sides only.

2. Crush the cookies into small pieces, then place in a bowl and mix with the butter, then compress into the base of the spring-form pan, set aside 4-ounces to the side for later.

3. Place in the fridge for 1 hour to chill.

4. Add all of your chocolate morsels to a stainless steel bowl, and place over simmering water for 15 minutes to melt them. Stir every so often.

5. Once melted, remove from the heat and place to the side.

6. In another bowl, beat the cream until it forms peaks and place in your fridge.

7. Beat the cream and sugar together in another bowl, when it is smooth, add the amaretto.

8. Gently blend in the whipped cream and chocolate.

9. Ladle the chocolate mix over the crumb mix in your spring-form pan and level it out.

10. Dust the top of the cake with 4-ounces of cookie mix.

11. Place in the fridge for 4 hours covered in cling wrap.

12. Remove the cake from spring-form pan and place on serving platter.

13. Serve with fresh strawberries and cream then enjoy!

Apple Cheesecake

I guarantee that you will really enjoy a big slice of this apple cheesecake!

Prep time: 20 minutes

Cook time: none

Chill time: 2 hours

Servings: 12 persons

Ingredients:

- 1 ¼ cup sugar
- 1-21 ounce can apple pie filling
- 1 teaspoon vanilla extract
- 6 tablespoons butter, melted
- 1 teaspoon cinnamon
- 8 ounces cool whip
- 2-8 ounces packs of cream cheese, softened
- 2 cups graham crackers, crushed

Directions:

1. Add your crushed crackers with butter and ¼ cup of sugar into a bowl and mix well.

2. Keep ¼ cup of the mix to one side and compress the remainder of the mix into a 9-inch spring-form pan.

3. Add the rest of your ingredients to a blender apart from the cool whip and pulse together.

4. Once mixture is smooth, slowly add the cool whip until fully combined.

5. Add the cake mix to the spring-form pan and level it out on top.

6. Place cake in your fridge for 2 hours.

7. Dust the top of the cake with the reserved cracker mix.

8. When ready, place on serving platter, slice and enjoy!

Peaches & Cream Cheesecake

This is a cheesecake recipe that you are sure to want to prepare again and again!

Prep time: 15 minutes

Cook time: none

Chill time: 4 hours

Servings: 16 persons

Ingredients:

- 1 cup sugar, divided
- 4-8 ounces packs cream cheese, softened
- 8-ounce pack whipping topping, thawed
- 2 cups graham cracker crumbs
- 2 peaches, fresh, chopped
- 6 tablespoons butter, melted
- 1-3-ounce pack of peach-flavored jelly

Directions:

1. Blend together the butter, crumbs and ¼ cup of sugar, compress mix into 9-inch spring-form pan.

2. Cream together the rest of the sugar with the cream cheese, then add the jelly powder and blend well.

3. Add the topping cream and peaches.

4. Evenly cover the biscuit base and place cake in your fridge for 4 hours.

5. Place on serving platter, slice, serve and enjoy!

Pistachio & Cherry Cheesecake

This cheesecake recipe is sure to delight the taste buds of those feasting at your table!

Prep time: 35 minutes

Cook time: none

Chill time: 4 hours

Servings: 8 persons

Ingredients:

For the crust:

- 12 graham crackers, crushed
- 1 stick of butter, melted

For the filling:

- green food coloring
- 1 cup cherry juice
- 1 cup sugar
- 1 cup of water
- 2 envelopes of gelatin
- ½ cup pistachios
- 4-8 ounces packs cream cheese

Directions:

1. Add your crackers to a blender and pulse with the melted butter until well combined.

2. Add the cracker mix to a 9-inch spring-form pan.

3. To make the cherry part of the cheesecake, add 1 gelatin pack to a bowl with ½ cup of sugar.

4. Heat the cherry juice and when it begins to a boil add to the gelatin and stir for about 5 minutes.

5. Take 2 packs of the cheese and beat until fluffy and creamy.

6. Mix in the gelatin and stir to combine.

7. Add the mix to your spring-form pan and place it in the fridge for 2 hours.

8. Add the other envelope of gelatin and remaining sugar into a bowl.

9. Heat 1 cup of water and when it boils, stir it into the gelatin, keep stirring until it melts.

10. Add pistachios to your blender and crush them into a paste.

11. Cream the remaining cheese with the pistachios and a little green food coloring.

12. Slowly mix in the gelatin until it is well combined.

13. Add this mix to the top of your cherry mix in the spring-form pan.

14. Place back into the fridge for 2 hours.

15. When the cake is firm, finish with whipped cream, serve and enjoy!

Chapter 3. Collection of Flavored Cheesecake Recipes

Pomegranate & Orange Cheesecake

This is a wonderful cheesecake recipe that you are sure to have over and over again!

Prep time: 20 minutes

Cook time: none

Chill time: 3 hours

Servings: 8-10 persons

Ingredients:

- 3 oranges, zest plus segments
- 3 tablespoons milk
- 21 ounces of full-fat cream cheese
- 3 ½ ounces icing sugar
- 3 1/2 ounces butter, melted
- 5 fluid ounces double cream
- 9 ounces digestive biscuits
- 1 whole pomegranate, seeds or 4-ounce tub

Directions:

1. Add your biscuits to a blender and pulse until they become crumbs, then place crumbs in a bowl.

2. Mix the melted butter into a bowl with crumbs. Add this mixture into a 9-inch spring-form pan and compress into the bottom.

3. Place into your fridge for 30 minutes to chill.

4. Beat sugar, milk, cheese, and zest in a bowl.

5. When well mixed, add your cream into a bowl and beat again.

6. Add the mixture over the biscuits in the spring-form pan, even mix out and place back into your fridge for 3 hours to chill.

7. Sprinkle the top of the cake with pomegranate seeds along with orange segments and zest.

8. Place on serving platter, slice, serve and enjoy!

Turtle Cheesecake with Brownie Base

Here is a special cheesecake recipe that is sure to put a smile on your face at the first bite!

Prep time: 35 minutes

Cook time: none

Chill time: 3 hours

Servings: 10 persons

Ingredients:

For the sauce:

- 3 tablespoons unsalted butter
- ¾ cup heavy cream
- pinch of salt
- 1 cup granulated sugar
- 1 teaspoon vanilla extract
- ¼ cup water

For the crust:

- 1 box of brownie ingredients and box ingredients
- For the cheesecake:
- ¾ cup caramel sauce
- ½ cup brown sugar
- pinch of nutmeg
- ½ cup granulated sugar
- 4 ounces cool whip
- ½ teaspoon cinnamon
- 16 ounces cream cheese, softened

For the topping:

- Hot fudge sauce
- caramel sauce
- chopped pecans

Directions:

1. Mix your brownie mixture and place into the bottom of a greased 9-inch spring-form pan.

2. Cook as per the directions on the brownie package.

3. Make your sauce by heating the sugar mixed with water, blending until melted.

4. Once sugar mix is melted, continue to cook until it starts to become a golden dark color, at this point do not stir, just move the pan around.

5. When you have reached the color that you desire, slowly add your cream into the pan once it stops bubbling stir mixture. Remove from heat and stir in the vanilla, salt, and butter.

6. Leave to one side, so it becomes thick.

7. In a bowl, cream the two sugars along with cream cheese, then add ¾ cup of sauce and spice.

8. Mix in the cool whip, blend to combine well.

9. Add the mix on top of the brownie mixture in spring-form pan and even out and place in your fridge for 3 hours.

10. Place cake on the serving platter, then drizzle with remaining sauce, hot fudge, pecans, then serve and enjoy!

Black Forest Cheesecake

This is a wonderful cheesecake recipe to serve at special meals as a yummy dessert!

Prep time: 20 minutes

Cook time: none

Chill time: 3 hours

Servings: 8 persons

Ingredients:

- 1 tablespoon confectioner sugar
- 1 cup sour cream
- 1-8-ounce pack cream cheese, softened
- 2 teaspoons vanilla extract
- 1-8-inch chocolate crumb crust
- 1/3 cup sugar
- ¼ cup of baking cocoa
- 1-21-ounce can cherry pie filling
- 1-8-ounce carton frozen whipped topping, thawed

Directions:

1. Cream together the sugar and cream cheese in a bowl, so it becomes smooth.

2. Whisk the sour cream and vanilla together with the cream cheese and gently blend in the whipped topping.

3. Place one half of mixture into the crumb crust and even out.

4. With the remaining mixture, add the confectioners' sugar and cocoa and blend together.

5. Spread over the top of the first mix and place in the fridge for 3 hours.

6. Place on serving platter, slice, serve with some cherry filling on top and enjoy!

Mixed Berry Cheesecake

This cheesecake recipe will delight the taste buds of all, especially the berry lovers!

Prep time: 35 minutes

Cook time: 90 minutes

Chill time: 10 hours

Servings: 12 persons

Ingredients:

For the crust:

- 6 tablespoons unsalted butter, melted
- 1 tablespoon sugar
- 1 ½ cups of graham cracker crumbs

For the filling:

- 1 ½ teaspoons vanilla extract
- ¼ cup sour cream
- 2 large egg yolks, room temperature
- 2 ½ pounds of cream cheese, room temperature
- 5 large eggs, room temperature

For the topping:

- ½ pint fresh strawberries
- ½ pint fresh blueberries
- 1 cup red jelly
- ½ pint fresh raspberries

Directions:

1. Heat your stove to 350° Fahrenheit.

2. Blend your sugar, crumbs, and butter, once they are well combined, press them into a 9-inch spring-form pan and 1-inch around the edge of the sides.

3. Cook in the oven for about 8 minutes, then remove from the oven, allow to cool.

4. Turn up the heat to 450° Fahrenheit.

5. Beat your sugar and cream cheese until they become fluffy.

6. Slowly add your eggs and eggs to the mix one at a time and mix in between.

7. Once your eggs are blended, add the zest, vanilla, and sour cream, and mix well.

8. Place into your spring-form pan and cook for about 15 minutes, then lower the heat to 225° Fahrenheit, and cook for an additional 75 minutes.

9. Once done, turn the heat off and then open the oven door, leave the cake for 30 minutes.

10. Remove cake from oven and allow to rest for 2 hours.

11. Place cake in the fridge and chill for 8 hours covered in cling wrap.

12. Place the cake onto a serving platter.

13. Warm the jelly in a small pan and add the berries and mix well. Drizzle mixture over your cheesecake. Slice, serve and enjoy!

Conclusion

I would first like to give you my thanks and appreciation for purchasing my collection of cheesecake recipes book. Cheesecake is a popular choice for many people when serving a special dessert that is not complicated to prepare but taste like it was something only a chef could create! I wish you many years of happy preparation of cheesecakes and may you take these recipes and make them your own by adding special ingredients to them that will suit your own special taste! Before you know it, you are going to be known for your yummy cheesecake delights! Friends and loved ones will soon be requesting their favorite cheesecake of yours that they can look forward to sharing with you on a special get together—and let's face it sharing a big slice of cheesecake is a great way to celebrate! Happy cheesecake baking and keep safe out there too!

Contributions to the book made by:

Pics supplied by Pinterest

About the Author

Nancy Silverman is an accomplished chef from Essex, Vermont. Armed with her degree in Nutrition and Food Sciences from the University of Vermont, Nancy has excelled at creating e-books that contain healthy and delicious meals that anyone can make and everyone can enjoy. She improved her cooking skills at the New England Culinary Institute in Montpelier Vermont and she has been working at perfecting her culinary style since graduation. She claims that her life's work is always a work in progress and she only hopes to be an inspiration to aspiring chefs everywhere.

Her greatest joy is cooking in her modern kitchen with her family and creating inspiring and delicious meals. She often says that she has perfected her signature dishes based on her family's critique of each and every one.

Nancy has her own catering company and has also been fortunate enough to be head chef at some of Vermont's most exclusive restaurants. When a friend suggested she share some of her outstanding signature dishes, she decided to add cookbook author to her repertoire of personal achievements. Being a technological savvy woman, she felt the e-book realm would be a better fit and soon she had her first cookbook available online. As of today, Nancy has sold over 1,000 e-books and has shared her culinary experiences and brilliant recipes with people from all over the world! She plans on expanding into self-help books and dietary cookbooks, so stayed tuned!

Author's Afterthoughts

Thank you for making the decision to invest in one of my cookbooks! I cherish all my readers and hope you find joy in preparing these meals as I have.

There are so many books available and I am truly grateful that you decided to buy this one and follow it from beginning to end.

I love hearing from my readers on what they thought of this book and any value they received from reading it. As a personal favor, I would appreciate any feedback you can give in the form of a review on Amazon and please be honest! This kind of support will help others make an informed choice on and will help me tremendously in producing the best quality books possible.

My most heartfelt thanks,

Nancy Silverman

If you're interested in more of my books, be sure to follow my author page on Amazon (can be found on the link Bellow) or scan the QR-Code.

https://www.amazon.com/author/nancy-silverman

Printed in Great Britain
by Amazon